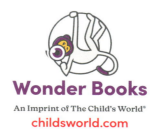

**Wonder Books**
An Imprint of The Child's World®
childsworld.com

**Published by The Child's World®**
800-599-READ • www.childsworld.com

**Copyright © 2023 by The Child's World®**
All rights reserved. No part of this book may be reproduced or utilized in any form or by any means without written permission from the publisher.

**Photography Credits**
Photographs ©: Shutterstock Images, cover, 2, 8, 14 (explosions), 14 (mountains), 14 (airplane), 19, 31; iStockphoto, 5, 25, 29; Olena Lialina/iStockphoto, 6; US Department of Energy/Flickr, 10, 15, 26; Tommy Stock Project/Shutterstock Images, 12; John Carnemolla/Shutterstock Images, 17; George Sheldon/Shutterstock Images, 21; Ryu Seungil/iStockphoto, 22

**ISBN Information**
9781503858091 (Reinforced Library Binding)
9781503860117 (Portable Document Format)
9781503861473 (Online Multi-user eBook)
9781503862838 (Electronic Publication)

**LCCN** 2021952448

**Printed in the United States of America**

## ABOUT THE AUTHOR

Clara MacCarald is a freelance writer with a master's degree in ecology and natural resources. When not parenting her daughter, she spends her time writing nonfiction books for kids.

Nuclear waste is dangerous to living things.

# TABLE OF CONTENTS

**CHAPTER ONE**
## RADIOACTIVE DOGS...4

**CHAPTER TWO**
## THE POLLUTION OF WAR...9

**CHAPTER THREE**
## NUCLEAR POWER AND WASTE...15

**CHAPTER FOUR**
## ACCIDENTS...20

**CHAPTER FIVE**
## TACKLING NUCLEAR POLLUTION...24

Fast Facts...28
Marble Chain Reaction...29
Glossary...30
Ways You Can Help...31
Find Out More...32
Index...32

# RADIOACTIVE DOGS

In 2019, a dog with long, brown fur slipped out of the bushes. Her name was Beta. She was hungry. She passed by a sign for the Ukrainian city of Chernobyl. The nearby buildings were all empty. But Beta knew where to find some humans who might have food.

No one lived in the city of Chernobyl anymore because of the **pollution** caused by a **nuclear** power plant. In 1986, part of the nuclear power plant in Chernobyl blew up. **Radioactive** pollution poured into the air. People living in the area escaped. They could not take their dogs with them. People also could not return for their pets.

People were evacuated from Chernobyl because of the danger of nuclear pollution.

The government created a zone that was off limits to most people due to **radiation** in the area. The zone covered 1,000 square miles (2,590 sq km).

Some dogs survived and had puppies. More than 30 years later, Beta was one of hundreds of dogs roaming the empty streets of Chernobyl. People could not live there, but they could tour the zone. Beta headed for a group of visitors. One man stepped back.

Dogs in Chernobyl can be contaminated by radiation.

Some of the dogs had radiation in their fur. He was afraid to touch her.

A woman approached Beta. The woman belonged to a group called the Clean Futures Fund. The group ran a program to take care of the dogs of Chernobyl. When Beta let the woman get close, the woman caught her.

## THE PETS OF FUKUSHIMA

In 2011, a nuclear accident happened at a plant in Fukushima, a city in Japan. Radiation forced people to leave their homes. Many of them left animals behind. Some people braved the threat of radiation to rescue hundreds of pets.

A vet checked Beta for radiation and found she was safe. Beta received a mark and a tag to identify her. The vet gave Beta medicine to keep her safe.

The dogs also faced other dangers. The zone was full of wild animals. Some had illnesses they could pass to other animals. Predators like wolves could kill dogs. The cold winters were hard. Few dogs survived to the age of six.

The people from Clean Futures returned Beta to the streets of the abandoned city. It was against the law to remove most things from the zone, even living creatures.

The government did not want to spread radioactive pollution. The Clean Futures Fund was allowed to rescue some puppies. For other dogs, like Beta, the polluted lands of Chernobyl would remain their home.

Nuclear pollution is radioactive pollution. It can come from nuclear weapons or nuclear power. As early as the 1940s, nuclear pollution began to affect the Earth's land, water, and air. But people have worked hard to clean up nuclear pollution. They have also worked to limit the danger of future accidents like Chernobyl.

Nuclear power plants are used to create electricity. However, power plants can cause nuclear pollution.

CHAPTER TWO

# THE POLLUTION OF WAR

On July 16, 1945, scientists gathered in the New Mexico desert. They were running the world's first test of a nuclear bomb. Some people thought the weapon might not work. It was a ball of metal filled with a radioactive **element**.

A nuclear **chain reaction** began inside the bomb. Radioactive **atoms** split apart. As each atom split, energy was released. Pieces from one atom caused other atoms to split, one after the other. Scientists saw a huge flash of light. There was a fireball, and then radioactive matter shot into the sky. The matter formed a giant cloud shaped like a mushroom.

In 1945, the first nuclear bomb was named "The Gadget."

The test had been a success. But the cloud moved to other areas. Some radiation in the atmosphere reached as far as New York. Close to the test site, radioactive fallout dropped from the sky. Fallout is radioactive dust that falls from the air when a nuclear bomb explodes. The nuclear blast had been bigger than scientists expected. The fallout had also reached a lot farther than they predicted. People did not know what the hot flakes were.

Animals died, and the fallout polluted the water and soil.

High doses of radiation can lead to radiation sickness in people. At first, radiation sickness makes people feel sick and throw up. Over time, they can lose hair. People often grow even sicker and die.

Lower doses of radiation can increase the chance a person will get cancer. People who lived close to the first nuclear bomb test had higher than normal rates of cancer.

Eventually, more countries got their hands on nuclear weapons. Making these weapons creates nuclear waste. Liquid used to process nuclear bomb fuel becomes radioactive. So do parts of the factories that make the weapons. Over time, radioactive matter becomes less radioactive. Some types become harmless in hours. But others can take tens of thousands of years. In 2021, the United States was still dealing with waste from making bombs in the 1900s.

People can become sick if they are exposed to radiation.

Once countries had nuclear weapons, they wanted to test them. So people exploded nuclear bombs in the atmosphere, on the mainland, and on islands. Some tests happened underwater or underground. In all, there were more than 2,000 tests.

## HIROSHIMA AND NAGASAKI

In August 1945, during World War II (1939–1945), nuclear weapons were used in war for the first and last time. The United States bombed two cities in Japan, Hiroshima and Nagasaki. More than 200,000 people may have been killed by the nuclear bombs. Those who survived witnessed terrible scenes. Many died afterward from burn wounds or radiation. Japan gave up a few days after the second bomb, ending the war.

Exploding nuclear bombs polluted the air, soil, and water with radioactive waste. Radiation entered people's food supply. Plants took up radioactive elements. Animals such as cows ate the polluted plants. Similar problems happened in the oceans.

Testing above ground ended in 1980. The radioactive pollution may have led to hundreds of thousands of cancer cases. Pollution also remained at old testing spots and in the oceans.

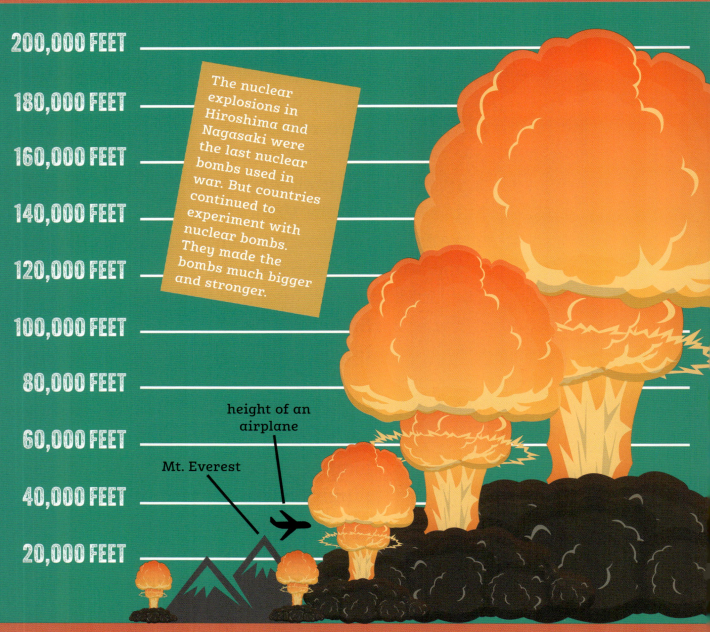

CHAPTER THREE

# NUCLEAR POWER AND WASTE

Like nuclear weapons, nuclear power plants use energy from nuclear chain reactions. The chain reactions take place in something called a reactor. Inside the reactor, atoms split and produce heat. The plant uses the heat to make electricity. In 2020, the United States had 96 nuclear reactors. The reactors produced about 20 percent of the electricity the country made every year.

It takes many workers to keep nuclear power plants running.

The reactors use a chemical element called uranium for fuel. Uranium is a radioactive element used to make nuclear energy. Uranium can be found underground. People can mine it in different ways. They can dig a pit or a deep tunnel. Miners take out rocks that contain uranium. Another way to get uranium is to pump chemicals underground. The chemicals remove the uranium from the rock. Then people pump the liquid back up.

## URANIUM MINES ON NAVAJO LANDS

In 1944, the United States started mining uranium on many different lands of the Navajo Nation. Navajo miners worked for low wages. They were not told about the dangers of radiation. Miners suffered many cases of lung cancer. After mining on the Navajo Nation's land ended, more than 500 old mines still remained. Radiation lingered in homes and in groundwater. The US and Navajo governments are still working to clean up the nuclear pollution.

Mining uranium adds to nuclear pollution.

The unwanted rocks and liquid left behind by mining and processing uranium into fuel are often radioactive. Although the radiation levels are low, they are still dangerous. People can cover the waste with clay and rocks. In the past, people piled the waste and left it behind. Wind blew radioactive dust into the air. And rain washed the pollution underground into drinking water.

Mining and processing uranium require a lot of energy. So does building a nuclear power plant. Some sources of this energy create air pollution. Many power plants burn fuel to make electricity. Burning pollutes the air. But when a nuclear plant is running, it does not produce any air pollution.

Running a nuclear power plant produces radioactive waste. The most radioactive waste comes from the plant's reactor. When the fuel for the reactor can no longer produce enough power to use, it is called spent fuel.

Many power plants store the spent fuel in concrete and steel containers. Spent fuel is extremely hot. It also has a deadly amount of radiation. Spent fuel stays radioactive for a very long time. It will still be able to kill people in 250,000 years. However, the container that holds the spent fuel is safe enough to touch. People have been shipping spent fuel for about 50 years without accidents.

Spent fuel needs to be stored safely.

## CHAPTER FOUR

# ACCIDENTS

Nuclear plant accidents are rare. But they create great dangers. A nuclear power plant accident is not like a nuclear bomb. The uranium does not explode. Instead, the reactor melts down. This can cause huge amounts of radioactive pollution. The most famous accidents include those at Three Mile Island, Chernobyl, and Fukushima.

Three Mile Island was a nuclear power plant in Pennsylvania. In 1978, machine problems and human mistakes caused a reactor to overheat. Part of the reactor melted down. Radioactive elements leaked into the air. Radiation levels rose around the plant. Fortunately, no one was hurt. However, the accident made people more fearful of nuclear power.

Chernobyl in 1986 is considered the worst nuclear accident. Workers were running a test on a reactor. They made several mistakes. For example, they shut down several safety systems. There was no nuclear explosion, but part of the reactor exploded. At least two people died.

Radioactive elements from the Chernobyl explosion spread far and wide. Radiation even reached as far as the United Kingdom. People tried to stop the nuclear reaction. They dumped things like sand and clay into the reactor. After much effort, workers closed the reactor off with cement and steel.

In 2021, the government was still trying to clean up radioactive waste from the accident at Three Mile Island.

The 2011 earthquake in Japan caused damage not only to buildings and homes but also to the nuclear plant in Fukushima.

Within a few months, at least 28 people had died of radiation sickness. The accident polluted a huge area. It forced about 200,000 people to move. Some plants and animals had mutations, or grew in strange ways. Cancer cases in children increased.

The second-worst nuclear power plant accident happened in 2011. A major earthquake struck the coast of Japan. This created a giant wave of water that hit a nuclear plant in Fukushima. The plant lost power. Safety systems failed. Three reactors started to melt.

The melting reactors created leaks. Leaking gas exploded. Radioactive matter began to pollute the surrounding area. To stop the pollution, workers pumped water and chemicals into the reactors. It took several months to completely cool the reactors.

The surrounding towns became unsafe. The government ordered people living close to the plant to leave. More than 100,000 people had to leave their homes. After time passed, the government let people return to some areas in Fukushima. Other areas still had too much radiation even by 2021.

Another kind of nuclear accident has involved submarines with nuclear reactors or weapons. One famous accident happened on a Russian submarine in 1961. The reactor got too hot. Radioactive steam surrounded the sailors who worked to keep the reactor from fully melting down. Radiation killed 22 of the men within the next two years.

CHAPTER FIVE

# TACKLING NUCLEAR POLLUTION

In 1959, scientists discovered radioactive pollution in wheat and milk. This made people concerned about nuclear testing. So in 1963, the United States and the Soviet Union signed a treaty. A treaty is a written agreement between countries. The treaty banned all nuclear weapons tests except those underground. Later, 71 countries signed a treaty that banned all nuclear weapons testing. Only India, Pakistan, and North Korea continued with tests.

With the rapid spread of nuclear weapons, people also feared nuclear war. If nuclear war broke out, there would be an immediate loss of life. It would also pollute huge areas.

People all over the world are worried about using nuclear weapons and power.

A treaty in 1970 managed to limit the number of countries that owned nuclear weapons. The treaty also allowed countries to share peaceful uses of nuclear power.

People are still cleaning up nuclear waste from more than 75 years ago. For example, the US government has been putting some waste underground. In 2020, the government buried nuclear waste in Carlsbad, New Mexico. The site has a deep hole in a bed of salt. The salt helps contain pollution from the waste.

People can carefully remove nuclear waste with the help of machines.

When people close a nuclear plant, they must deal with the radiation danger. This process is called decommissioning the plant. Burying a nuclear power plant in concrete is one way to close it down.

Other ways to decommission a plant aim to make the area free of radioactive matter. The quickest way is for workers to remove anything radioactive from the plant.

There is also a longer method, which allows the reactor and machines to stay at the plant for many years. The material becomes less radioactive before workers take it away.

Nuclear accidents have led to some important lessons. People started to look at better safety systems. They worked to improve training for the workers operating the plant. Governments planned how to quickly respond to problems that might occur. People learned similar lessons from Chernobyl, Three Mile Island, and Fukushima.

Nuclear pollution is an important concern. However, it is not the whole story of nuclear power. Nuclear plants make a lot of electricity every year in the United States. It is a cleaner choice than using coal or oil, which produces more air pollution. Nuclear power has many possible benefits for the future of Earth.

## FAST FACTS

- The first nuclear bomb exploded on July 16, 1945, in a New Mexico desert. Radioactive pollution from the bomb spread to surrounding areas.

- Nuclear bombs work by causing nuclear chain reactions. An atom splits, giving off huge amounts of energy, and bits of that atom cause other atoms to split and continue the process.

- High doses of radiation can cause radiation sickness and death. Lower doses can increase someone's risk for cancer.

- Creating and testing nuclear weapons cause radioactive pollution.

- Accidents at nuclear power plants are rare but can create great dangers. Famous accidents include the ones at Three Mile Island, Chernobyl, and Fukushima.

- When a nuclear power plant is decommissioned, or closed down, people must remove or secure all the radioactive matter at the plant.

- Nuclear power has many benefits. Once the fuel is in the reactor, nuclear power plants can produce a lot of electricity without polluting the air.

# MARBLE CHAIN REACTION

## MATERIALS
- 10 marbles
- 2 wooden blocks

### DIRECTIONS

1. A nuclear bomb has radioactive atoms very close together. Gather your ten marbles. Put nine marbles close together on the floor.

2. Roll the tenth marble into the others. Watch what happens. Imagine every marble that is hit is also split apart.

3. A nuclear reactor has the radioactive atoms more spread out. Spread the nine marbles out. Try rolling your one marble into the marbles.

4. Special rods in nuclear reactors take in some of the atom bits to slow the chain reaction. Spread the nine marbles out again. This time, while you roll your marble, try stopping some of the marbles with the wooden blocks to slow the reaction. How does each change affect the results?

# GLOSSARY

**atoms** (AT-uhms) Atoms are extremely tiny particles that are building blocks of all matter in the universe. Humans are made up of atoms.

**chain reaction** (CHAYN ree-AK-shuhn) A chain reaction is a line of events in which each action causes new actions. A chain reaction is needed for a nuclear weapon to work.

**element** (EL-uh-muhnt) An element is a basic substance made from a single atom. Gold is an element.

**nuclear** (NOO-klee-ur) Nuclear means having to do with the power produced when atoms split. People use nuclear power for energy.

**pollution** (puh-LOO-shuhn) Pollution is something harmful that is added to the air, land, or water. Nuclear pollution is unsafe to be around.

**radiation** (ray-dee-AY-shuhn) Radiation is when energy moves through waves or particles. Radiation is a big concern when a nuclear power plant has an accident.

**radioactive** (ray-dee-oh-AK-tiv) Radioactive means something has atoms that give off radiation. The dogs in Chernobyl are radioactive.

# WAYS YOU CAN HELP

- Learn about any nuclear activity in your area, such as old testing spots, uranium mines, and nuclear power plants.

- Talk to friends and family about nuclear pollution.

- Write letters to government officials about nuclear weapons.

# FIND OUT MORE

### In the Library

Bell, Samantha S. *How Can We Reduce Nuclear Pollution?* Minneapolis, MN: Lerner Publications, 2016.

Brallier, Jess. *What Was the Bombing of Hiroshima?* New York, NY: Penguin Workshop, 2020.

Honders, Christine. *Nuclear Power Plants: Harnessing the Power of Nuclear Energy.* New York, NY: PowerKids Press, 2018.

### On the Web

Visit our website for links about investigating nuclear pollution: **childsworld.com/links**

Note to Parents, Teachers, and Librarians: We routinely verify our Web links to make sure they are safe and active sites. So encourage your readers to check them out!

# INDEX

animals, 4–8, 11, 13, 22

Chernobyl, 4–8, 20, 21, 27

fallout, 10–11

Fukushima, 7, 20, 22–23, 27

nuclear testing, 9–13, 21, 24

power plants, 4, 7, 15, 18, 20, 22–23, 26–27

sickness, 11, 16, 22

Three Mile Island, 20, 27

uranium, 16–18, 20